D0759245

Who Says?

Who Says?

Written by Kirsten Hall and Jessica Flaxman

Illustrated by Wayne Becker

My First READER

children's press®

A Division of Scholastic Inc.
New York Toronto London Auckland Sydney
Mexico City New Delhi Hong Kong
Danbury, Connecticut

Library of Congress Cataloging-in-Publication Data

Hall, Kirsten.
  Who says? / written by Kirsten Hall and Jessica Flaxman ; illustrated
by Wayne Becker.– 1st American ed.
        p. cm. – (My first reader)
Summary: Singing before a musical conductor, animals from chicken to owl
reveal their own special sounds.
  ISBN 0-516-22958-3 (lib. bdg.)   0-516-24642-9 (pbk.)
  [1. Animal sounds–Fiction. 2. Singing–Fiction. 3. Stories in rhyme.]
I. Flaxman, Jessica. II. Becker, Wayne, ill. III. Title. IV. Series.
  PZ8.3.H146Wh 2003
  [E]–dc21
                                    2003003697

Text © 1990 Nancy Hall, Inc.
Illustrations © 1990 Wayne Becker
Published in 2003 by Children's Press
A Division of Scholastic Inc.
All rights reserved. Published simultaneously in Canada.
Printed in the United States of America.

1 2 3 4 5 6 7 8 9 10 R 12 11 10 09 08 07 06 05 04 03

Note to Parents and Teachers

Once a reader can recognize and identify the 16 words
used to tell this story, he or she will be able to read successfully
the entire book. These 16 words are repeated throughout the story,
so that young readers will be able to easily recognize
the words and understand their meaning.

The 16 words used in this book are:

bark	horse
chicken	neigh
cluck	of
course	owl
croak	quack
dog	says
duck	the
frog	who

Cluck says the chicken.

Cluck, cluck, cluck.

9

Who says *quack?*

Of course, the duck!

Bark, bark, bark.

Bark says the dog.

Who says *croak*?

Croak says the frog.

Neigh, neigh, neigh.

Neigh says the horse.

25

Who says *who?*

The owl, of course!

ABOUT THE AUTHORS

Kirsten Hall has lived most of her life in New York City. While she was still in high school, she published her first book for children, *Bunny, Bunny*. Since then, she has written and published more than sixty children's books. A former early education teacher, Kirsten currently works as a children's book editor.

Jessica Flaxman, a graduate of Wesleyan University, is pursuing a Ph.D. in literature at Columbia University. Her nonfiction work has been published in the San Francisco *Chronicle* and *Newsday*. Flaxman lives with her husband and baby in New York City.

ABOUT THE ILLUSTRATOR

Wayne Becker was born in Chicago, Illinois. After earning degrees at Northwestern University and the University of Michigan, he studied art at the School of Visual Arts in New York. Becker has been illustrating books and working in animation for more than thirty years. He lives in rural upstate New York with his wife, who was his high-school sweetheart, and his dog.